Little Elm Community Library
Little Elm, TX 75068

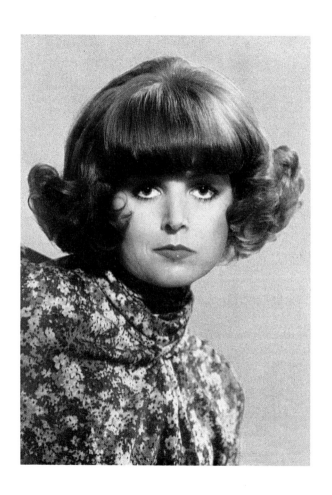

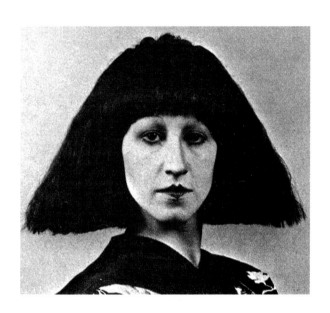

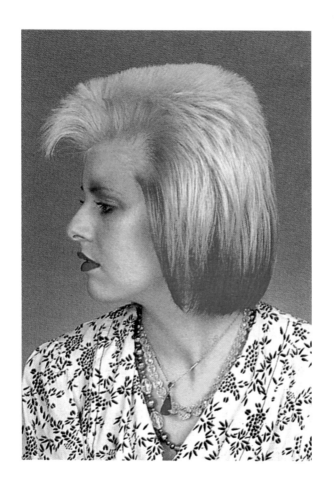

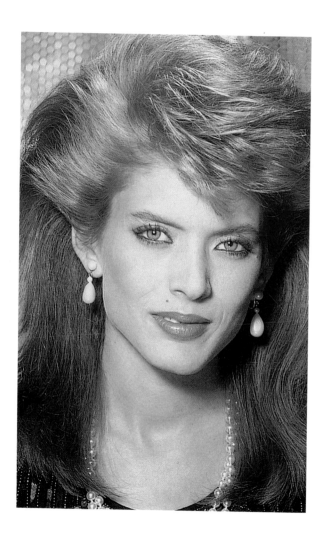

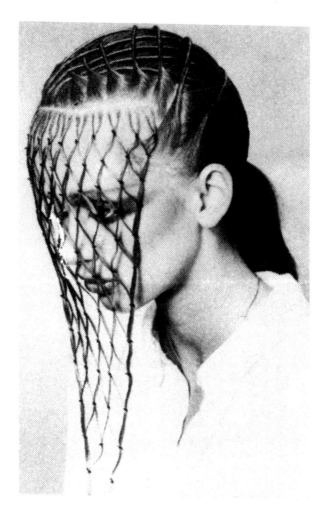

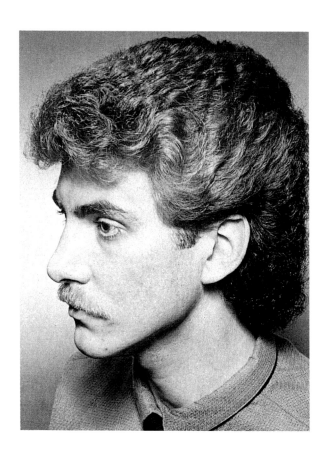

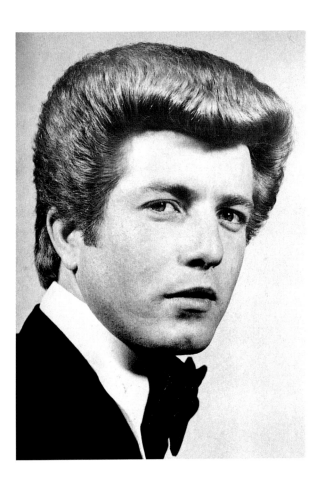

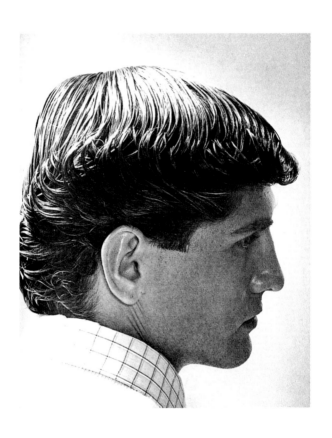

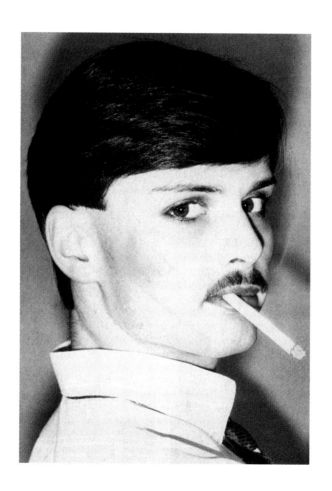

PUBLISHED BY BLOOMSBURY, NEW YORK AND LONDON
DISTRIBUTED TO THE TRADE BY HOLTZBRINCK PUBLISHERS

ALL PAPERS USED BY BLOOMSBURY ARE NATURAL,
RECYCLABLE PRODUCTS MADE FROM WOOD GROWN IN
SUSTAINABLE, WELL-MANAGED FORESTS. THE
MANUFACTURING PROCESSES CONFORM TO THE
ENVIRONMENTAL REGULATIONS OF THE COUNTRY OF ORIGIN.

ISBN 1-58234-449-3

FIRST U.S. EDITION 2003

10 9 8 7 6 5 4 3 2 1

PRINTED IN SINGAPORE BY TIEN WAH PRESS

BIG HAIR
BY JAMES INNES-SMITH

DESIGNED BY NATHAN BURTON

WITH SPECIAL THANKS TO JOHN SUETT AT PROJECT PHOTOGRAPHY, HENRIETTA WEBB, MARY DAVIS AND THE LIBRARY AT THE LONDON COLLEGE OF FASHION.

CREDITS: CHRISTOPHA, REGENTS PARK ROAD; ROUGH CUTS, ISLINGTON